Raccoon on the Moon

Russell Punter

Illustrated by David Semple

"Goodbye!" cries Raccoon.
"I'm off to the moon.

I'll be back by lunchtime,
or late afternoon."

Goose grins and she giggles.

You foolish Raccoon!

3, 2, 1...

BOOM!

He zooms into space.

Far up to the stars,
at a fabulous pace.

He reaches the moon.
But SMASH! What a shock.

His craft crashes BUMP
on a sharp lump of rock.

The ship hits the ground.
It's split down one side.

Now I might be
stuck here.

Raccoon bounds
outside...

"My name is Zack. I live on the moon.

Give me your hand and
I'll have you back soon."

Zip's buggy chugs up.

He whips out a tool.

Fizz! goes his gizmo.

The ship is fixed.

Cool!

They bound by a crater...

climb mountains...

see valleys...

until, three
hours later...

The ship
reaches Earth.

"Three cheers for Raccoon!"

His chums greet their hero.

You've been to the moon!

About phonics

Phonics is a method of teaching reading used extensively in today's schools. At its heart is an emphasis on identifying the *sounds* of letters, or combinations of letters, that are then put together to make words. These sounds are known as phonemes.

Starting to read
Learning to read is an important milestone for any child. The process can begin well before children start to learn letters and put them together to read words. The sooner children can discover books and enjoy stories and language, the better they will be prepared for reading themselves, first with the help of an adult and then independently.

You can find out more about phonics on the Usborne Very First Reading website, **www.usborne.com/veryfirstreading** (US readers go to **www.veryfirstreading.com**). Click on the **Parents** tab at the top of the page, then scroll down and click on **About synthetic phonics**.

Phonemic awareness

An important early stage in pre-reading and early reading is developing phonemic awareness: that is, listening out for the sounds within words. Rhymes, rhyming stories and alliteration are excellent ways of encouraging phonemic awareness.

In this story, your child will soon identify the *oo* sound, as in **soon** and **zoom**. Look out, too, for rhymes such as **bump** – **lump** and **high** – **cry**.

Hearing your child read

If your child is reading a story to you, don't rush to correct mistakes, but be ready to prompt or guide if he or she is struggling. Above all, do give plenty of praise and encouragement.

Edited by Jenny Tyler and Lesley Sims
Designed by Sam Whibley

Reading consultants: Alison Kelly and Anne Washtell

First published in 2015 by Usborne Publishing Ltd., Usborne House, 83-85 Saffron Hill, London EC1N 8RT, England.
www.usborne.com Copyright © 2015 Usborne Publishing Ltd.